Haunted in Alabama

Compiled By

Marie Tayse

CONTENTS

Foreword
Alabama
Buck Creek Cotton Mill
Main Street Strip
Blockbuster
Marion Military Institute
Jemison – Van de Graaff Mansion
USS Alabama BB – 60 Battleship
Sloss Furnaces
Adams Grove Presbyterian Church
Battle House Hotel & Spa
Old Bryce Hospital
Drish House
Gaineswood
Sweetwater Mansion
Huntingdon College
St. James Hotel
Gaines Ridge Dinner Club
Harrison Cemetery
Tutwiler Hotel
Jack Cole Road
Redmont Hotel
Fort Morgan
Hudson House
Rawls Hotel
A WORD OF THANKS
A GIFT OF THANKS
Resources
Other Books By This Author

Foreword

Paranormal by definition means something that is not scientifically explainable. So, according to that definition, ghosts, angels, demons, shadow figures, etc. are considered to be paranormal. Cryptids, such as Bigfoot, the Loch Ness Monster, the Jersey Devil, El Chupacabra, and the Yeti are also thought to be paranormal or 'beyond the norm'. In addition, aliens, elementals, and banshees are paranormal. However, for the books in this series we will be focusing solely on locations where entities or beings are responsible for the phenomenon that has been occurring.

For more information about the paranormal and to read eyewitness encounters and some of the cases Seeking Answers Paranormal of Tennessee has worked, check out my book A Walk Into the Unknown, available on Kindle & Kindle Unlimited, Paperback, and Audiobook.

The locations in this book are all actively haunted. If you decide to pay a visit to any of these locations, please adhere to signs posted on or around the grounds. Be sure to have permission from the owner before entering private property. Trespassing is not condoned for any reason.

Alabama

Native Americans lived in present-day Alabama long before the Europeans arrived. The Cherokee, Choctaw, Creek, Chickasaw, Coushatta, and Yuchi Tribes all once called the area home. The Europeans arrived in the sixteenth century, and they soon began exploiting the land and resources of the Natives. Alabama became a state on December 14, 1819. In 1830, the majority of the Native Americans in the area were forcibly removed from their homelands and sent to live on reservations to make room for cotton plantations and other American expansions. Today only a small number of Choctaw and Creek Tribes remain in Mobile, Washington, Atmore, and Escambia Counties.

African American slave trade began once the Native Americans were gone, and by 1860 the slave population consisted of nearly half of the entire state population. Alabama joined the Confederacy in January 1861. Abraham Lincoln's Emancipation Proclamation freed over three million slaves in the Confederate states in January 1863.

The largest Civil War battle to occur in Alabama was in Mobile and Baldwin Counties in August 1864. It is now known as the Battle of Mobile Bay. More than 1800 causalities occurred, with the majority being on the Confederate side.

From 1915 to 1930, thousands of the state's African Americans joined the Great Migration and moved from the Southern states to better opportunities in the North. From the 1954 to 1968, Alabama played a big part in what is now known as the Civil Rights Movement. During that time, the state saw numerous acts of violence against African Americans, including church bombings and a variety of actions by the Ku Klux Klan. On December 1, 1955, Rosa Parks made history by refusing to give up her seat to a white man on a bus in Montgomery, Alabama. Her courageous stand prompted the year-long Montgomery bus boycott. Ten years later, she rode one of the first desegregated buses in the state.

On September 14, 1969, the Talladega Speedway opened. By the 2000s, it would attract thousands of racing fans to the state each year. On March 17, 1970, what is now known as the U.S. Space and Rocket Center in Huntsville was dedicated.

Alabama averages about twenty-two tornadoes a year, but some years have seen many more. The state is part of what is known as Dixie Alley, coming in second to Tornado Alley with the most tornadoes in the United States. Recently, Dixie Alley has had more deadly tornadoes than Tornado Alley in the plains states. The year 2018 saw forty-six tornadoes here. In 1932, 270 people were killed in Alabama in fifteen tornadoes that touched down in the span of two days in March. During the 1974 Tornado Outbreak, seventy-seven lives were lost in seven Alabama counties. On April 27, 2011, 132 people were killed when sixty-two tornadoes ravaged the state.

Alabama's nickname is the Heart of Dixie. As of 2010, it had a population of 4,779,736. Its state insect is the Monarch Butterfly, and the state reptile is the Alabama Red-Bellied Turtle. The state capital is Montgomery, and its largest city is Birmingham. Average highs in August range from 93 degrees Fahrenheit in Tuscaloosa to 88 degrees Fahrenheit in Coden. Average lows in January range from 46 degrees Fahrenheit in Dauphin Island to 31 degrees Fahrenheit in Decatur.

Buck Creek Cotton Mill

The Buck Creek Cotton Mill in Alabaster, Alabama opened in 1896. It was built in an area that was the location of the Creek War of 1836, a conflict that occurred between the United States Army and the Creek Nation. Several deaths happened in the area as a result of the war. The mill was renamed a few times before becoming the Buck Creek Cotton Mill in 1911. It was shut down in 1979. In 2003, the city bought the property and tore down many of the buildings surrounding the mill. In 2010, a Senior Citizens Center was built on part of the original mill property.

According to locals, dark shadows have been seen outside of the remaining mill buildings. Cold spots and strange noises have also been experienced. Dark stains resembling blood can be seen on the floor of one of the buildings, according to multiple sources.

Permission from the city is required to access the property. The local police will prosecute trespassers.

Main Street Strip

Main Street in Albertville, Alabama runs both East and West through the center of town, which is what is locally called 'the Main Street Strip'. In April 1908, an EF-4 tornado struck the strip killing fifteen (some sources said eighteen) and injuring more than a hundred. Businesses and homes along the strip were or nearly leveled. They were later rebuilt and the survivors in Albertville tried to move on, but those who lost their lives that day were apparently not at rest and remain that way today.

Many current and past Main Street Strip business owners and local townsfolk insist that the spirits of the tornado victims remain where they died. A sudden coldness can be felt in spots along the strip, even during the summer months. Disembodied voices and footsteps can be heard when no one is near. The screams of people are often heard at night when the street and businesses are empty.

(The destruction left behind by the tornado.)

(The Main Street Strip today.)

On April 24, 2010, an EF-3 tornado again hit downtown Albertville, but thankfully no one was killed.

Blockbuster

In May of 2002, two employees and two customers were shot execution-style inside the Blockbuster store in Anniston, Alabama. The victims were Douglas Edward Neal Jr, 27, Austin Carl Joplin, 23, and brothers Joseph Michael Burch, 20, and Andrew Robert Burch, 19. Their killer, Donald Wheat, was sentenced to death, but died in prison before he could be executed. The store closed after the murders and never reopened. The families of the victims placed four crosses out front in their memory. The building was later turned into a doctor's office.

There are claims of the new business and the property of being haunted, possibly by the victims of the murders. Shadows, cold spots, and feelings of being watched have all been experienced. A quick cool breeze with no apparent cause can sometimes be felt.

Marion Military Institute

The Marion Military Institute in Marion, Alabama was built in 1842 as part of Howard College. During the Civil War, the Chapel and Lovelace Hall were used as a military hospital. The ground behind the Chapel was used to bury the dead. Until World War II, the institute's campus consisted of only two buildings, but today the Marion Military Institute has thirty buildings covering over 160 acres.

There are tales of at least two suicides on the campus, but this could not be confirmed. The number of casualties in the makeshift hospital during the Civil War is unknown.

Cadets and others on the campus claim to have heard strange banging and dragging noises, felt as though they were being watched when no one else was around, and heard their name being called when they were alone.

Others have complained of their personal belongings disappearing, having their clothing tossed from their dressers, and smelling of strange out-of-place odors.

Jemison – Van de Graaff Mansion

The Jemison – Van de Graaff Mansion was built in 1859 in Tuscaloosa, Alabama by Senator Robert Jemison Jr. It was the first house in the area to have a bathroom with indoor plumbing. In the 1940s, the property changed hands and restoration began on the mansion. During the time from when it was built to the 1950s, the house was the private residence of multiple families. From 1955 to 1979, the house served as the Friedman Public Library. Then in 1991, preservation and restoration began on the property to bring it back to its original condition. Today, portions of the mansion and grounds are available to the public for weddings, parties, and receptions.

During the Civil War, a man by the name of Andrew Hargrove was shot in the head, but survived. However, he suffered from severe headaches as a result of his injuries. On December 6, 1895, in the Jemison Mansion where he resided with his wife, he committed suicide in the library. Some believe his spirit is one of several roaming around inside the mansion.

Visitors and residents of the property have claimed to have feelings of being watched, hearing strange unearthly music echoing throughout, and seeing objects being thrown. Crashing sounds with no apparent cause are also heard inside the mansion. The apparition of a girl has been seen on the main staircase.

USS Alabama BB – 60 Battleship

The USS Alabama BB – 60 Battleship began its career in 1943 during World War II. During its time at sea, the ship was home to 2,500 crewmen. It earned nine battle stars and the nickname the 'Mighty A'. After four and a half years of service, the USS Alabama was retired. In 1965, the ship was opened to the public at the USS Alabama Battleship Memorial Park in Mobile, Alabama. The ship was also used for filming the movie USS Indianapolis: Men of Courage.

While the ship was at sea no crew members died from enemy fire, however, two men were killed during the ship's construction, along with the deaths of five men by accidental friendly fire on February 21, 1944. Eleven others were wounded that day.

Over the years many visitors to the 680 – foot long ship have reported paranormal activity and unexplained occurrences. There have been claims of hearing footsteps as though someone is walking toward you when there was no one there. Popping and tapping noises have been heard in the bulkheads with no known cause. Other activity onboard the ship includes: feelings of being watched, apparitions being seen, orbs having both been seen and captured in photographs, whispering has been heard, steel hatches slam shut on their own, and a lady has had her earrings tugged on.

Sloss Furnaces

Construction of Sloss Furnaces in Birmingham, Alabama began in June 1881. The Whitwell stoves were the first of their type to be built in Birmingham. They stood sixty feet tall and were eighteen feet in diameter. In April 1882, the furnaces began operation. Within its first year, the company sold 24,000 tons of iron. Founder James Sloss retired in 1886 and sold the company to a group of financers, who began rapid expansions. By World War I, Sloss Furnaces were among the largest producers of iron in the world. In 1981, they were designated as a National Historic Landmark, and then in 1983 the complex opened as a museum. Today the property consists of two 400 – ton blast furnaces and forty other buildings, however, nothing remains of the original complex. The oldest building still standing today dates back to 1902.

Several deaths occurred through the years at the furnaces. Most of their names and causes of death have been lost throughout history, however, a few are known. On February 4, 1892, an accident with a scaffold occurred, resulting in the deaths of John Staton and John Ritchie, as well as the injuries of five others. On August 4, 1897, a young boy discovered the body of a white male in an open water tank on the property. The man was later identified as Joseph Webb, who had last been seen at a bar the night before. It is unknown whether his death was an accident or if he was murdered. In October 1906, James "Slag" Wormwood either lost his balance and fell or was pushed into a pit of melted iron ore. Stories differ on whether he or someone else was at fault.

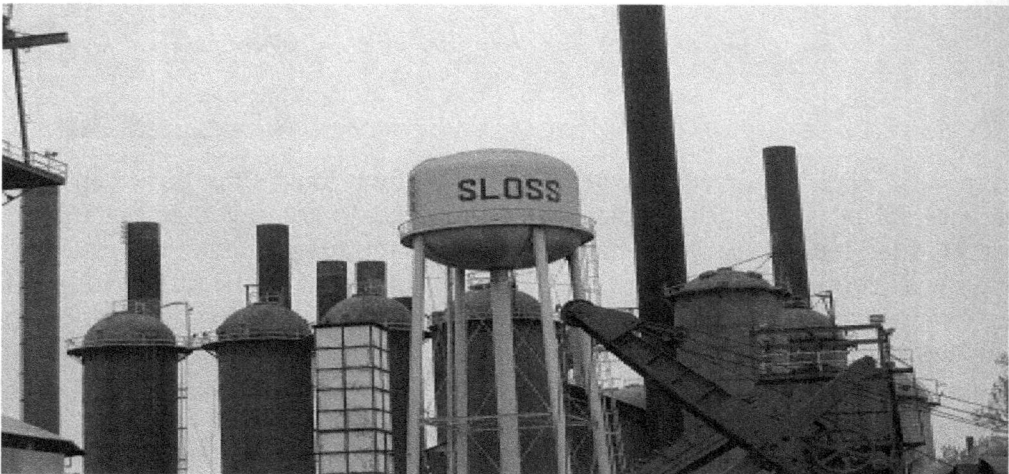

Both employees and visitors to the furnaces have reported numerous paranormal and unexplained occurrences. Some of the accounts may be based in legend, but it is believed by many that most claims are factual.

In 1947, three workers were attacked by an apparition of a man with severe burns. In 1971, a night watchman was assaulted by an entity he described as being half man / half demon. Steam whistles are often heard, as well as the appearance of strange shapes, shadow figures, and other apparitions.

Adams Grove Presbyterian Church

The Adams Grove Presbyterian Church near Sardis, Alabama was built in 1853. It shares its grounds with the Adams Grove Cemetery. The building is one of the few pre-Civil War churches still standing in the area. There were church services held there until 1974. On June 5, 1986, it was added to the National Register of Historic Places. The property is now privately owned.

Visitors and parishioners have reported feeling overwhelming sadness on the grounds. The apparition of a Confederate soldier has been seen ordering people off the property, and a shadow man with red eyes has given some quite a scare. An apparition believed to be a former minister is occasionally seen inside the church during thunderstorms, and a crying baby can be heard when no children are near.

Battle House Hotel & Spa

The Battle House Hotel & Spa in Mobile, Alabama was built in 1908 on the site of the original Battle House Hotel that burned down in 1905. The first hotel opened in 1852. The location was also the site of an old military headquarters set up by Andrew Jackson during the War of 1812. The new hotel was renovated both in 1916 and again in 1949. The hotel closed in 1974, and remained closed for the next thirty years. In 1975, the building was added to the National Register for Historic Places. In 2003, restoration began on both the hotel and its adjoining skyscraper office building. The Battle House Hotel reopened on May 11, 2007, and the spa opened in 2009.

A man named Henry Butler was allegedly beaten to death in Room 552 by the husband of his lover. There are some tales of a woman committing suicide in the hotel in 1910, but neither her name nor the confirmation of her death could be found. There were no deaths in the fire of the original structure, although 147 guests were displaced.

During the renovations of the hotel, the workers' tools would go missing seemingly of their own accord. Sometimes they would complete a project only to return the following day to find it back to the condition it had been in before, as though they had only imagined completing it to begin with. Some believe the ghost of Mr. Butler to haunt the fifth floor near where he was supposedly murdered. Many guests and employees have reported faucets and lights turning on and off by themselves, hearing unexplained noises and disembodied voices, and seeing wispy figures throughout the hotel. Other

Haunted In Alabama

claims of ghostly activity in the hotel includes bright flashes of light with no source, shadowy figures appearing in mirrors and other wall hangings, and something unseen lying down in the beds of unsuspecting guests.

Old Bryce Hospital

What is known as the Old Bryce Hospital was built in the 1850s in Tuscaloosa, Alabama, and opened in 1861 as the Alabama State Hospital for the Insane. The hospital's first physician was Dr. Peter Bryce. He and his wife lived in a house on the grounds until his death in 1892. He was buried on the property. Eight years later, the state officially renamed the facility Bryce Hospital in his honor. Little more is known about the property until 2010, when the University of Alabama bought the grounds and began a major restoration project. Once the project is completed, the hospital buildings will be used as a university welcome center, a museum of mental health, a museum of the university's history, event space, and classrooms for performing arts students.

Some sources say that while Dr. Bryce himself prohibited the use of inhumane treatments and devices, such as shackles and straitjackets, after his death the patients were subjected to horrific abuse and neglect. The number of deaths at the hospital is unknown. Only the name of one patient who died at the hospital is known. A young boy is believed to have died there while undergoing a type of hydro-therapy (basically water boarding) to calm his hyperactivity. Mary Lou Smith died on November 1923 of tuberculosis. She had been admitted in June 1922 suffering from dementia. She is one of what has been estimated to be over 3,000 people buried in four sites on the grounds of the Bryce Hospital. Patients who died there were buried with a marker etched with a number, not their name. In addition, when the Jack Warner Parkway was built in the 1960s, several of the graves were either relocated or lost.

The apparition of a young boy has been seen on the grounds. There are both hot and cold spots in the building. Disembodied screams and footsteps can be heard; and there are claims of objects disappearing on their own.

Drish House

The Drish House in Tuscaloosa, Alabama was built in 1837 in the middle of a 450 - acre plantation owned by Dr. John Drish and his wife Sarah. After both of their deaths, the house changed hands several times before being purchased by the Tuscaloosa Board of Education. The Jemsion School opened there in 1906. It remained a school until 1925, when it was bought to be used as a parts warehouse for a local wrecking company. In 1940, the house was once again sold; this time it was to be used as a church. The house was in a state of disrepair by 2006, when it was added to the Alabama Historical Commission. The additions to the house by the renovations made when it was a church were demolished in 2009. In 2012, renovations began on the house, and in 2016, it opened as an event venue. Weddings, receptions, and parties are now held at the house.

The only death known to have occurred in the house was that of Dr. Drish in 1867 after he fell down a stairwell. Sarah died in 1884, but it is not known if her death occurred on the property or not.

Many people throughout the years have reportedly seen a fire in the third-story tower, even though no evidence of a fire could be found. Claims of seeing lights coming from the house when there should not have been any have also been reported.

Gaineswood

A house called Gaineswood in Demopolis, Alabama was constructed over an eighteen year period between 1843 and 1861. Most of its construction was completed by slaves. It was once the center of a large plantation. A two-room cabin originally sat on the site. The home's first owner, Nathan Whitfield, died in 1868, leaving it to his son, Bryan Whitfield. In 1923, the house was sold to the Kirven family. After that it changed hands several additional times until it was purchased by the state in 1967. In 1975, the house was opened to the public as a historic house museum.

Nathan Whitfield's first wife, Elizabeth, died on the property in 1846 of unknown causes. Another woman passed away inside the home from pneumonia a few years later, but sources differ on her name. Information on whether or not there were other deaths on the property could not be confirmed.

Residents and visitors to the home have reported seeing ghostly shadows. The sounds of a piano, as well as disembodied footsteps can be heard at times throughout the house.

Sweetwater Mansion

Sweetwater Mansion, also known as the Governor Robert Patton House, in Florence, Alabama was built in 1835. The home basement once served as a Civil War hospital, and it may have also been used as a county jail at one time. Further history of the mansion is unknown.

While no information regarding any deaths on the property could be found, there were several funerals held in the house. Most notably was the wake for Billy Patton, Governor Patton's son who was killed while fighting for the Confederacy in the Battle of Shiloh. Some believe that the bodies of two of the Governor's sons killed in the war are buried beneath the floorboards inside the house.

The paranormal activity in the mansion has been witnessed by everyone from the caretaker to paranormal investigator teams. Ghostly whispers, footsteps, and the sounds of children laughing when none are present have all been heard. Objects have been known to move on their own accord. The apparition of a woman dressed in 19th century clothing and shadow figures have seen around the property. A caretaker even experienced the replay of a decades past funeral.

Huntingdon College

Huntingdon College in Montgomery, Alabama was originally founded in 1854 in Tuskegee, Alabama, as a white woman-only college. In 1872, the school faced closure due to economic issues during the Civil War. To prevent this, the Alabama Conference of the Methodist Episcopal Church took over the school and renamed it the Alabama Conference Female College. In 1909, it was moved from Tuskegee to Montgomery. That same year, the school was renamed the Women's College of Alabama. In 1910, a fire in one of the college's buildings destroyed all of its records. The school admitted its first male student in 1934, and it was renamed Huntingdon College the following year.

Only one death is known to have occurred on the current campus. Martha (or Margaret, sources differ) committed suicide in her room after weeks of becoming increasingly withdrawn.

The tales of paranormal activity at Huntingdon College has both grown and changed throughout the years, but the majority of both faculty and students believe there spirits roaming the grounds from years past. The most often reported sighting is that of the lady in red, thought by some to be Martha (or Margaret). The 'red lady' apparition is seen casually strolling about the fourth floor of Pratt Hall. Some students have claimed to have heard a faint breathing in their ear or had their clothing tugged on at night while walking on the green.

Haunted In Alabama

The apparitions of a young boy and a female student wearing only a towel have also been seen around campus.

St. James Hotel

The St. James Hotel in Selma, Alabama was built in 1837 and opened soon after as The Brantly, named after General John Brantly. At some point prior to the Civil War, the hotel was renamed The Troupe House. In 1871, the hotel was renamed once more to the St. James Hotel. The property changed hands several times before closing its doors in 1893. Between then and 1997 when restoration began on the property, the building was used for numerous commercial and business purposes. The hotel reopened after the restorations were completed. In 2017, it once again closed down, and by September of that year the doors and windows were being boarded up. It is not known whether or not it has yet to reopen or if it will.

There are no confirmed deaths on the property, but that does not stop both guests and employees from seeing the apparitions of whom many believe to be Jesse James and his girlfriend Lucinda. Both were regulars at the hotel in life. The spirit thought to be Jesse is often seen in the rooms he normally occupied when he was alive, as well as, sitting at one particular table in the bar. The apparition believed to be Lucinda is usually seen walking the halls. Some have reported to having been able to smell the lavender perfume she frequently wore. The phantom barks of a dog are also heard throughout the building.

Gaines Ridge Dinner Club

The Gaines Ridge Dinner Club in Camden, Alabama was built in 1827. The family of Reverend Ebenezer Hearn was the original owners of the property. In 1898, the family of Mrs. Betty Gaines Kennedy purchased it. It remained a private residence until 1985 when Mrs. Betty and her sister opened the Gaines Ridge Dinner Club. The restaurant remains in operation under the same owners today.

It is unknown if any deaths occurred on the property, but both employees and guests have experienced paranormal activity in the building. One of the owners has heard a female voice calling out to her when no one present had done so. On one occasion, several guests heard what they believed to have been a woman fall inside the lady's room, but upon investigation there was no one there and nothing to account for the sounds. Some have smelled the aroma of pipe smoke in the front room, and the cries of a baby can occasionally be heard coming from an upstairs room.

Harrison Cemetery

Harrison Cemetery in Kinston, Alabama is thought to be haunted by William "Grancer" Harrison, also known as "the dancing ghost". Grancer Harrison was born in 1789 in Edgefield, South Carolina and moved to Coffee County, Alabama in the 1830s. He was a wealthy plantation owner, and he was known locally for his parties and his love of dancing. When he died in May 1860 at the age of seventy-one, he was buried inside a tomb on the property that later became known as Harrison Cemetery. Several claim to have seen Grancer's apparition dancing alongside his tomb to the ghostly sounds of a fiddle.

Tutwiler Hotel

The Tutwiler Hotel in Birmingham, Alabama was originally built in 1914 on the corner of 20th Street and 5th Avenue North. It was thirteen stories with 425 rooms. It closed in 1972. In 1974, the original hotel was demolished and First Alabama Bank built in its place. In 1986, the new Tutwiler Hotel reopened in what had been the Ridgely Apartments on Park Place, a few blocks over from where the old hotel had stood. The new owner included a fitness and business center, modern guest rooms, and a signature restaurant with the new location. In 2006, the hotel was purchased by a different company and renovations were done. In April 2007, the hotel became part of the Hampton Inn & Suites brand. It is now called The Tutwiler Hampton Inn & Suites.

It is unknown if there were ever any deaths on the property before it became The Tutwiler, but there have not been any to date since. Nonetheless, staff and guests continue to encounter two apparitions in the building. The first of which is an unidentified male spirit who is known to rapidly knock on the doors of guests staying on the sixth floor in the middle of the night. Another spirit has been known to turn lights and appliances on and off. The latter is believed to be Major Tutwiler himself.

Jack Cole Road

Jack Cole Road in Hayden, Alabama is known as one of the state's most haunted roads. Since 1890, over seventy people have died along this unpaved road. Sixty-eight of those deaths were due to a cholera outbreak at a hospital that once stood along Jack Cole Road. In the 1940s, the mummified remains of an elderly woman were found in a house along the same road. In the 1960s, a man was found murdered in a house at the end of the road. He had been bludgeoned to death with an ax. In 2003, a male resident of Jack Cole Road told friends that he had begun to see strange things in and around his house. He passed away only a few days later. On February 5, 2015, fifty-two year old Felicia "Lisa" Weaver was at the home she shared with her son on Jack Cole Road when it caught fire. Her son had gone to run errands. She was on oxygen and in very bad health. She was unable to care for herself, and she could not have left the home without help. When the fire was extinguished, the bodies of the family's three dogs were found in the ashes but Lisa has never been seen again. The cause of the fire remains unknown.

(Interesting tidbit: I researched Lisa's case for my book The Missing, but I had no idea at the time that the road on which she resided and disappeared from had such a creepy past.)

Some locals believe Jack Cole Road is cursed by a witch that once made her home in the area. Whether or not you believe that theory, it seems very odd that so many deaths (and a disappearance) could occur on one unpaved road surrounded by woods without some explanation. Throughout the years there have been reports of strange lights in the trees, loud unexplainable noises, and apparitions walking alongside the road.

Redmont Hotel

The Redmont Hotel in Birmingham, Alabama first opened in 1925. In 1946, the hotel was purchased by a businessman named Clifford Stiles. The following year, he converted the entire top floor into a penthouse apartment for him and his family. He died in 1975, and from there the hotel began to decline. In 1983, it was purchased by an investment group and added to the National Register of Historic Places. After a renovation, the hotel reopened in 1985. Another renovation was done in 2000. In 2014, the hotel underwent a multimillion-dollar restoration. On March 8, 2016, the Redmont Hotel reopened as part of the Curio Collection by Hilton brand. It now consists of eleven floors with 120 guest rooms.

While no evidence can be found to confirm or deny any deaths occurring in the building, there seem to be many who enjoyed their stay at the Redmont so much that they returned after death. Country music singer Hank Williams Sr. is one spirit that began making appearances right after he died. Clifford Stiles is also believed to have remained behind in the hotel he once called home. Those two are thought to be behind the disembodied footsteps, doors opening and closing by themselves, strange sounds, and baggage and furniture that seemingly moves on its own. Both of their apparitions have been seen, as well as the apparitions of a woman in a white dress on the ninth floor and a small dog.

Fort Morgan

Fort Morgan in Gulf Shores, Alabama was preceded by Fort Bowyer in 1813 to guard against British attacks during the War of 1812. Construction of Fort Morgan began in 1819 and was completed in 1834. Seventeen men of the Confederate army were killed on August 22, 1864, when the Union artillery bombarded the fort. Beginning in 1895, the United States Corps of Engineers began construction of a new fortification system to protect against that happening again. During World War I, two thousand troops were stationed at Fort Morgan. But by July 1944, it was abandoned.

With such a history of death and violence, most people could see how it has such an abundance of paranormal activity. While some visitors have not had any experiences at all on location with the otherworldly, others have claimed to have in some way felt the presence of those who never made it home from the war. Ghostly voices and footsteps have been heard. Apparitions and unexplained lights have been seen, and some have witnessed a replay of a long ago battle.

Hudson House

The Hudson House in Ashland, Alabama was built in the early 1900s. The Hudson family lived in the home until John Hudson died in 1966. The history of the house after that has been lost to time. It is on private property.

No evidence could be found regarding any deaths on the property, but by the amount of reported paranormal activity it stands to reason that something in its past caused it to become steeped in ghosts. There are reports of people being tapped on the shoulder while standing in the front yard. Disembodied voices, footsteps, and the sound of the front door opening and closing when in reality it did not have all been reported. A dog has often been heard panting or growling, and a dark figure has been seen on the roof.

Rawls Hotel

The Rawls Hotel in Enterprise, Alabama was built in 1903 by Captain Japheth Rawls. The building was remodeled in 1928, and three-story wings were added by Jesse P. Rawls. The hotel closed in the early 1970s. It was added to the National Register of Historic Places in 1980. Today, the hotel operates as a bed and breakfast.

It is unknown whether or not there were any deaths in the building, but since as far back as the end of World War I numerous individuals have reported paranormal activity there. The playful laughter and apparitions of children have been witnessed throughout the hotel. Disembodied voices, sounds of glass breaking, gasping or raspy breathing, ghostly music, crashing and banging sounds, running water, footsteps, giggling, and unexplained knocks have all been heard at some point in the building. Apparitions, shadows, and what is believed to be Captain Rawls' spirit have been seen in various areas around the property. Paranormal investigators have recorded EVPs and captured spirits in photographs. Objects have been known to move by themselves, phantom smells have often wafted through the second and third floors, and feelings of being watched have been experienced.

Haunted In Alabama

If you enjoyed reading this first book in the Truly Paranormal series, be sure to follow me on Facebook, Smashwords, Amazon, Goodreads, or Twitter to hear about new releases in this series. The links to do this are below.

Marie Tayse Facebook Author Page

Marie Tayse Smashwords Profile

Marie Tayse Amazon Author Page

Marie Tayse Goodreads Author Profile

Marie Tayse Twitter

A WORD OF THANKS

I sincerely hope you enjoyed reading this book, and I thank you for purchasing it. If you don't mind, I would really appreciate you going over to the site that you bought it from and leaving a rating and review. As an indie author, it is difficult to get my books in front of people without the ratings and reviews of readers like you.

Thanks Again,

Marie Tayse

A GIFT OF THANKS

As a thank you for purchasing this book (and hopefully becoming a new fan of my books), I would like to offer you the opportunity to purchase two of my other books for FREE. All you have to do is click on the links below, and then once you are redirected click Buy Now. As always, I would very much appreciate it if you will leave a rating and review of each after you read them. Below are the titles (with links), genres, and descriptions of each. Again, I want to thank you for taking the time and choosing to read my books out of all of the millions of others that are out there to choose from. It means so much!

The First Case (Colt Investigations #1)

Paranormal Fiction

A teen who takes on the emotions of those around him. A child that sees visions of events to come. A loving, devoted father and husband who seems to become a totally different person overnight. An older brother who knows something is not quite right at home. An elderly neighbor that sees shadow figures in the windows of the house next door. A best friend who is convinced a demonic entity is responsible for nearly all of the events.

From the street no one can see the horrors unfolding inside. People driving and walking by are completely unaware of the pure evil lurking just beyond the porch.

Billy Colt doesn't believe in the paranormal. While he accepts that some people have extraordinary abilities, any talk of the possibility that ghosts or demons may be responsible for the unexplainable events plaguing his family is totally absurd in his opinion. But when a horrific murder takes place, leaving even the local police at a loss, he is forced to rethink his beliefs. With the help of his brother and best friend, Billy begins an investigation of his own. What he eventually discovers will change his entire way of thinking and set the stage for what his life's work will be.

The Greatest Gift

Contemporary Romance

Daniel has never been anything but a burden to all who knew him. He's got big dreams, but no one will look far enough past his autism diagnosis to see them. Candace grew up in a home where she never felt like she was good enough. As soon as she could, she moved out to California to make a new life for herself. One day the two cross paths, and from that moment on neither of their lives are ever the same. Together they set out on a daring adventure across the country where they find unconditional love in the most unlikely of places.

Resources

o https://www.currentresults.com/Weather/Alabama/temperature-january.php
o https://statesymbolsusa.org/states/united-states/alabama
o https://www.history.com/topics/us-states/alabama
o https://www.weather.gov/bmx/event_04272011
o https://en.wikipedia.org/wiki/1974_Super_Outbreak
o https://en.wikipedia.org/wiki/1932_Deep_South_tornado_outbreak
o https://www.weather.gov/bmx/tornadodb_main
o https://www.cnn.com/2019/03/05/us/dixie-alley-tornadoes-southeast-wxc/index.html
o http://www.sercc.com/education_files/tornadoes_al.pdf
o https://www.archives.alabama.gov/timeline/al1951.html
o https://www.history.com/topics/civil-rights-movement/civil-rights-movement-timeline
o https://en.wikipedia.org/wiki/History_of_Alabama
o https://www.civilwaracademy.com/civil-war-battles-in-alabama
o http://www.encyclopediaofalabama.org/article/s-142
o https://digitalalabama.com/alabama-ghost-towns/alabaster-old-buck-creek-cotton-mill/6534
o http://www.encyclopediaofalabama.org/article/h-3866
o https://sites.rootsweb.com/~gataylor/crkindw.htm#1836
o http://quadcitiesdaily.com/?p=336320
o https://www.weather.gov/bmx/event_04241908_dora
o https://www.pinterest.com/pin/547539267171146382/
o http://www.mystery411.com/Landing_oldblockbustervideostore-anniston.html
o http://www.ghoststoriesworld.com/haunted-houses-of-america/ghosts-from-anniston-blockbuster-murders
o http://www.encyclopediaofalabama.org/article/m-3384
o https://www.alabamasfrontporches.org/attraction/ghost-stories/
o https://marionmilitary.edu/about-mmi/history/
o https://www.hauntedplaces.org/item/marion-military-institute/
o http://www.jemisonmansion.com/history.html
o https://www.alabamapioneers.com/tuscaloosa-jemison-van-de-graaff/
o https://www.ussalabama.com/explore/uss-alabama-battleship/
o https://www.hauntedrooms.com/top-8-most-haunted-places-in-alabama
o https://www.navysite.de/bb/bb60.htm
o http://definition.org/most-haunted-places-in-alabama/

- https://www.slossfurnaces.com/history/
- http://www.lastgasps.com/page40.html
- http://www.frightfurnace.com/hauntings/haunted-history-of-sloss-furnace/
- http://www.mystery411.com/Landing_adamsgrovepresbyterianchurch.html
- https://en.wikipedia.org/wiki/Adams_Grove_Presbyterian_Church
- https://www.flickr.com/photos/152415490@N02/albums/72157688857255814
- https://www.onlyinyourstate.com/alabama/haunting-history-church-al/
- https://en.wikipedia.org/wiki/The_Battle_House_Hotel
- https://www.marriott.com/hotelwebsites/us/m/mobbr/mobbr_pdf/Battle%20House%20History.pdf
- https://www.onlyinyourstate.com/alabama/hotel-haunting-history-al/
- https://www.visitsouth.com/2016/01/12/the-haunted-history-of-the-battle-house-hotel/
- http://www.encyclopediaofalabama.org/article/h-1564
- http://hauntedhaven.blogspot.com/2014/12/bryce-asylum-tuscaloosa-and-northport.html
- http://blog.al.com/spotnews/2010/04/bryce_hospitals_deceased_are_n.html
- http://www.tuscaloosa-library.org/the-challenges-of-accessing-medical-records/
- http://www.historicdrishhouse.com/
- https://www.onlyinyourstate.com/alabama/haunted-house-al/
- https://en.wikipedia.org/wiki/Dr._John_R._Drish_House
- https://www.ruralswalabama.org/attraction/gaineswood-started-1842-completed-on-eve-of-civil-war/
- http://www.encyclopediaofalabama.org/article/h-3020
- https://fringeparanormal.wordpress.com/2013/09/11/the-paranormal-at-home-hauntings-in-50-states-alabamas-sweetwater-mansion/
- https://www.hauntedrooms.com/sweetwater-mansion-florence-alabama-haunted-ghost
- https://en.wikipedia.org/wiki/Sweetwater_Mansion
- http://www.encyclopediaofalabama.org/article/h-2378
- http://blog.al.com/strange-alabama/2012/04/the_red_lady_of_huntingdon.html
- https://en.wikipedia.org/wiki/Red_Lady_of_Huntingdon_College
- https://www.historichotelslodges.com/2018/05/the-saint-james-hotel.html
- http://blog.al.com/strange-alabama/2012/04/selmas_st_james_hotel_one_of_t.html

- https://www.selmatimesjournal.com/2017/09/20/st-james-hotel-boarded-up/
- https://www.ruralswalabama.org/attraction/gaines-ridge-dinner-club-1837/
- http://www.weirdus.com/states/alabama/stories/gaines_ridge_dinner_club/index.php
- http://blog.al.com/strange-alabama/2012/06/ghosts_history_and_great_food.html
- https://www.geni.com/people/William-Grancer-Harrison/6000000005097232673
- http://www.mystery411.com/Landing_harrisoncemeterykinston.html
- https://deepsouthmag.com/2014/12/03/100-years-of-history-at-birminghams-tutwiler-hotel/
- https://www.bhamwiki.com/w/Tutwiler_Hotel_(1986)
- https://www.southernthing.com/the-most-haunted-hotel-in-every-southern-state-2614406563.html?rebelltitem=1#rebelltitem1
- https://deepsouthmag.com/2014/12/03/100-years-of-history-at-birminghams-tutwiler-hotel/
- https://www.cartercompany.net/blog/haunted-happenings/
- http://www.serpentsofbienville.com/blog-index/2015/10/10/alabama-oddities-weekly-breakdown-october-5th-october-11th
- https://www.onlyinyourstate.com/alabama/haunted-al-road/
- https://www.amazon.com/Missing-True-Disturbing-Files-Book-ebook/dp/B07JMHVX2J/ref=sr_1_4_twi_kin_1?ie=UTF8&qid=1547185145&sr=8-4&keywords=marie+tayse
- https://styleblueprint.com/birmingham/everyday/13-bone-chilling-haunted-places-alabama/
- https://en.wikipedia.org/wiki/Redmont_Hotel
- https://www.wanderingsoulsapp.com/2017/07/23/haunted-redmont-hotel-birmingham-alabama/
- http://www.fort-morgan.org/history/
- https://www.sunsetproperties.com/blog/haunted-fort-morgan/
- https://www.britannica.com/place/Mobile-Bay
- http://www.oxfordparanormalsociety.com/hudsonhousefolklore.html
- https://digitalalabama.com/alabama-haunted-places/hudson-house-alabama/13839
- http://paranormalstories.blogspot.com/2011/05/hudson-house.html
- https://www.tripadvisor.com/Restaurant_Review-g30509-d566364-Reviews-Rawls-Enterprise_Alabama.html#photos;aggregationId=101&albumid=101&filter=7&ff=260231556

Haunted In Alabama

- https://www.facebook.com/pages/Rawls-Hotel/190853354443419
- https://www.greatest-unsolved-mysteries.com/haunted-places-in-alabama.html
- https://www.dothaneagle.com/enterprise_ledger/news/the-haunted-history-of-the-old-rawls-hotel/article_85aeeea2-9f71-11e6-ba4a-cf3cdfc719fd.html
- https://www.hauntedplaces.org/item/the-rawls-hotel/

Other Books By This Author

The Monster Within

The Protector

One Great Love

One Message

A Walk into the Unknown

The Greatest Gift

Meet Miracle (The Adventures of Miracle #1)

One Big Furry Family (The Adventures of Miracle #2)

Furry Holidays (The Adventures of Miracle #3)

The First Case (Colt Investigations #1)

This Nightmare Called Life (Colt Investigations #2)

Laid to Rest (Colt Investigations #3)

Haunted by Evil (Colt Investigations #4)

The Missing (True Disturbing Files #1)

The Unsolved (True Disturbing Files #2) **Coming Winter 2019**

Haunted In Alaska (Truly Paranormal #2)

Haunted In Arizona (Truly Paranormal #3)

Haunted In Arkansas (Truly Paranormal #4) **Coming March 2019**

Haunted In Alabama

Haunted In California (Truly Paranormal #5) **Coming April 2019**

Haunted In Colorado (Truly Paranormal #6) **Coming May 2019**

www.ingramcontent.com/pod-product-compliance
Lightning Source LLC
Chambersburg PA
CBHW030307030426
42337CB00012B/618